71 Great Places to Visit in North Wales: North Wales Travel Guide

71 Great Places to Visit in North Wales: North Wales Travel Guide

A local's guide to great places to visit in North Wales

Dylan Thomas

Table of contents

Introduction

Hello and thank you for choosing this guide to help you discover and enjoy all of the delights that North Wales has to offer!

The aim of this guide is not to cover every single thing that North Wales has to offer, but to focus on the things that I think are definitely worth exploring and enjoying.

The guide has been split into 4 sections:

Outdoors and Activities

Exploring

Castles

Food & Drink

The best way to use this guide is to check the locations on the maps in each section and review how these align with the types of activities that you are looking for.

Whatever you are looking for, there is definitely something for you to enjoy in beautiful North Wales.

Enjoy!

Outdoors and activities

This section of the book focuses on more active and activity based things to do in North Wales. For example, there will be a focus on all things thrill seeking and adventure finding.

The more energetic activities will be discussed and shown in this section. Whether you are an adrenaline junkie or like to keep two feet firmly on the ground, there will be something for you to enjoy in this section of the guide.

Map - Outdoors and activities

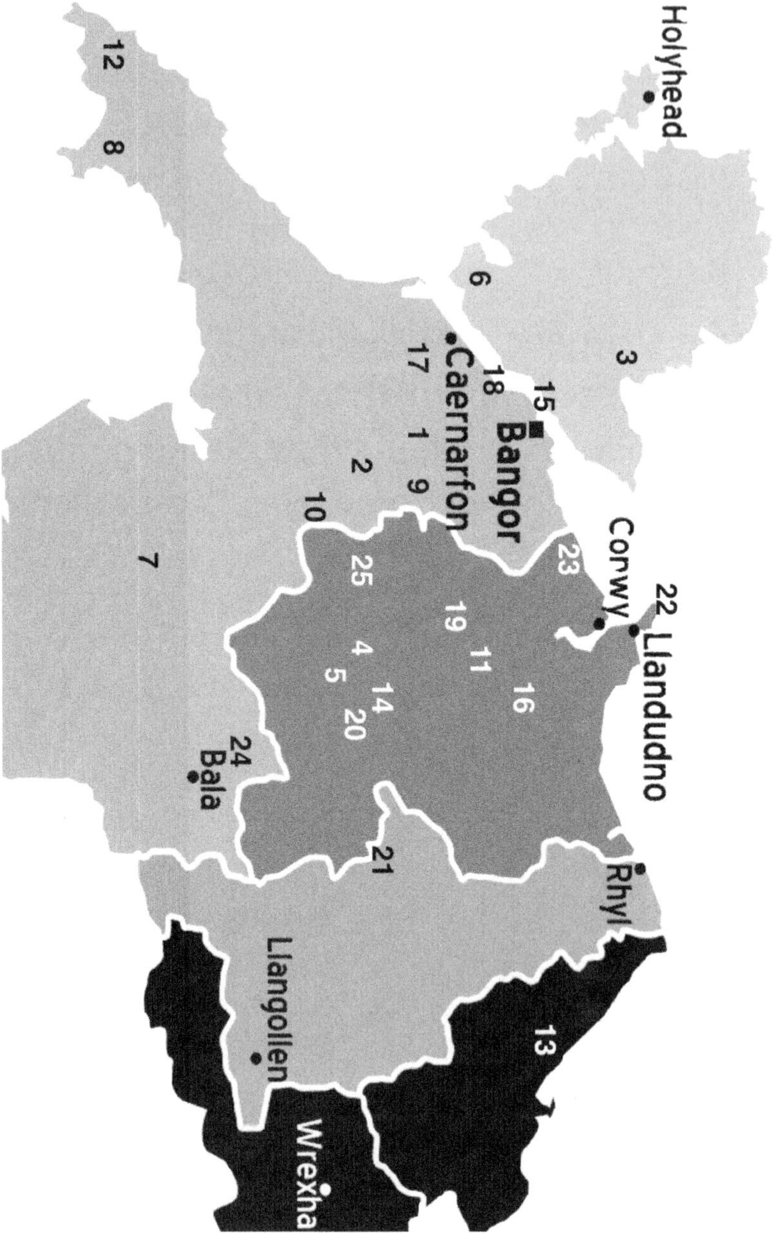

1. Paddle board on Llyn Padarn

The lake of Llyn Padarn sits beautifully in the heart of Snowdonia, with an amazing view of Snowdon. Paddle boards are available to hire near the car park by the lake, and these allow you to have a bit of fun on the lake! If you don't fancy paddle boarding, I'd highly recommend taking a dip in the lake under trees to the left of the car park or simply walking around the lake to take in the views. At the south of the lake there's the famous lonely tree, which makes for idyllic photographs of the surroundings.

WWW.SNOWDONIAWATERSPORTS.COM

2. Conquer Snowdon (Yr Wyddfa)

Snowdon, or Yr Wyddfa in Welsh, is the tallest mountain in Wales sitting at 3,560ft (1,085m) at its peak. If you're feeling up to it, it can be a hard 6-8 hour hike up and down. There are multiple routes up the mountain, but the 9 mile route route starting in Llanwrst I'd say is the most rewarding with the best views on the way up. The weather can change in an instant so make sure to go prepared, with sensible clothing and equipment. Try and time your walk on a day when the café is open at the summit as a reward. It can get very busy on the mountain during summer so it's best to get there as early as possible.

WWW.VISITSNOWDONIA.INFO/SNOWDON-WALKING-ROUTES

3. Anglesey Coastal Path

The Anglesey Coastal Path is a path that loops around the whole of Anglesey's coast, taking in many beautiful spots and nature reserves.The path passes through landscape that includes a mixture of farmland, coastal heath, dunes, salt-marsh, foreshore, cliffs and a few small pockets of woodland. Although the whole path is 130 miles, it can be broken down and tackled in much smaller sections. I'd recommend Red Wharf Bay to Fedw Fawr or Penmon as this can be completed in a circular walk.

WWW.VISITANGLESEY.CO.UK/EN/ABOUT-ANGLESEY/ISLE-OF-ANGLESEY-COASTAL-PATH/

4. Enjoy the surging Swallow Falls

Swallow Falls is a beautiful waterfall situated just outside Betws-y-Coed. The waterfall on the river Llugwy has become famous for its views. Although the main viewpoints are on the south bank of the Llugwy where there is also plenty of parking, the best view is definitely when approached on foot along the northern bank.

WWW.VISITSNOWDONIA.INFO/SWALLOW-FALLS

5. Take a hike up to Llyn Elsi

Llyn Elsi is situated above Betws y Coed with a fairly moderate but steep walk up to the lake. When walking up there are encouraging signs of how much further to go which really help with the walk and definitely help with how much further to go (No more "How much further?!?!"). I'd definitely recommend this as a lunchtime hike and to take a picnic to enjoy the views once at the top. It's not recommended to swim in the lake however as it can be dangerous.

WWW.VISITSNOWDONIA.INFO/LLYN-ELSI-BETWS-Y-COED

6. Take a dip at Newborough beach

Newborough (Llanddwyn) beach is a beautiful beach located on Anglesey's coastline. Stretching over a mile long, the beach is amazing on a summer day. There is a large car park directly next to the beach as well which can fill up on those extra busy weekends, so make sure to get there early to ensure a spot. The beach backs onto Newborough forest which is lovely to walk around and explore. The sea is also known for having consistent waves that can be great for surfing/ bodyboarding.

WWW.VISITWALES.COM/ATTRACTION/BEACH/LLANDDWYN-BEACH-1821332

7. Hire mountain bikes in Coed y Brenin

If you're feeling adventurous, Coed y Brenin is brilliant place to meet your adrenaline needs. Coed y Brenin was the first forest to be developed for the sport of mountain biking and still remains an excellent location for the sport. With a visitor centre that hires out bikes, there are trails suitable for all levels, whether you bring a bike with you or not.

WWW.BEICSBRENIN.CO.UK

8. Surf in Abersoch

Abersoch is home to one of the most popular beaches in Wales. Sitting on the Llŷn Peninsula, the beach provides an excellent venue for all things water sports, due to having no severe currents or riptides. The town also hosts annual jazz, regatta and music festivals and is home to plenty of great places to eat and drink.

WWW.ABERSOCHLIFE.COM

9. Take a ride on the fastest zipline in the world!

Located in the heart of Penrhyn Quarry, the Velocity 2 zipline is a must-do for all adventure seekers out there. The zipline can reach speeds of over 100mph, and with up to 4 people racing down the 1.5km line at once it can be an amazing thrill. Make sure to check out the other activities available at the zip world such as the quarry karts and enjoy the magnificent quarry views.

WWW.ZIPWORLD.CO.UK/ADVENTURE/VELOCITY

10. Extreme underground bouncy castle

Have you ever heard of an enormous trampoline situated in an underground cave and disused mine? No? Well look no further than Zip World Bounce Below, which houses a very unique experience which allows you to boudin your way through a huge hidden adventure. This place is fun for all ages, and definitely has to be seen to be believed.

WWW.ZIPWORLD.CO.UK/ADVENTURE/BOUNCE-BELOW

11. Never miss a wave at Adventure Parc Snowdonia

North Wales is very fortunate to house one of only two wave pools in the whole of the UK. Adventure Parc Snowdonia, formally Surf Snowdonia, is a 300m long pool that can create waves of up to 2m tall. Don't be put off though, as the wave pool caters to all abilities depending on which part of the pool you use. They provide surf lessons and also have a lot of other activities surrounding the pool to get involved in.

WWW.ADVENTUREPARCSNOWDONIA.COM

12. Go for a swim or a stroll on Porth Iago Beach

The sandy little cove of Porth Iago is one of the best beaches to be found on the Llyn Peninsula. Flanked by the low grassy headlands of Dinas and Graig Ddu, the beach here is pretty well sheltered making it a great spot for a dip in the clear blue waters. Porth Iago is accessible from one of the newest sections of the Wales Coast Path via a scramble down the dunes.

WWW.THEBEACHGUIDE.CO.UK/NORTH-WALES/GWYNEDD/PORTH-IAGO

13. Experience the healing waters of St Winefride's Well

St Winefride's Well has attracted visitors for 1300 years and is a dedicated Holy Shrine to Saint Winefride, it's also known as one of the Seven Wonders of Wales. It is the oldest unbroken pilgrimage site in Great Britain and a wonderful experience for anyone who goes to visit. The legend of Saint Winefride is definitely very interesting which I'd recommend reading about.

WWW.STWINEFRIDESWELL.ORG.UK

14. Zoom down the UK's only Alpine Coaster

The Zip World Fforest Coaster is an unbeatable adrenaline experience for anyone aged over 3. The track allows you to race through twisty turns and bends between trees. The toboggan like coaster is attached to rails and sits very close to the ground, allowing you to get a great sense of speed. The coaster can reach speeds of 25mph, though you can control the brakes so you can go as fast or slow as you like! Three goes are included with your tickets, allowing you to build up your courage!

WWW.ZIPWORLD.CO.UK/ADVENTURE/FFOREST-COASTER

15. Search for wildlife on a rib tour

Take a trip on a rib boat ride down the Menai Straits to explore the surrounding areas on a thrilling speedboat. You'll experience magnificent sights along the Menai Strait, and depending on which ride you choose, you may even get a chance to see some wildlife. Make sure to wrap up warm and waterproof as it can get cold out on the water.

WWW.RIBRIDE.CO.UK

16. Get lost in Bodnant Gardens

Bodnant Gardens is considered one of the great British Gardens, and is definitely a great day out for garden lovers and nature lovers. The 80 acres of gardens span meadows, woods riverside gardens and over 250 years of history. It's home to plants and trees and botanic collections from around the world. Enjoy daffodils, camellias, magnolias and rhododendrons in spring; roses, waterlilies, and wildflowers in summer; rich leaf colour in autumn; and a stunning, designed Winter Garden. You can easily spend at least 2 hours here.

WWW.NATIONALTRUST.ORG.UK/BODNANT-GARDEN

17. Take shelter from the rain in Beacon Climbing Centre

Rain or shine, come and climb! Beacon Climbing Centre is an exciting all-weather venue, with fun activities suitable for the whole family. The users are aged 4-80+ and the climbing is designed to cater for all levels. Conquer the high roped walls for an unbeatable sense of achievement, experience the freedom of climbing without using a rope in the low level bouldering areas or try something that's entirely off-the-wall: CrazyClimb featuring a series of wacky climbing challenges! No previous experience is required and anyone can have a go.

WWW.BEACONCLIMBING.COM

18. Get involved in Plas Menai activities

Plas Menai, the National Outdoor Centre for Wales is perfectly situated for the ultimate outdoor adventure. Its mission is to unleash the power of adventure. And it does exactly that. It offers action-packed activity days, whether you're looking to conquer a new skill of learn to wind surf, or simply looking for an exploring adventure in a kayak, chances are Plas Menai has something for you.

WWW.PLASMENAI.WALES

19. Walk up to Llyn Eigiau

Llyn Eigiau lies in a glaciated valley on the edge of the Carneddau mountain range. It's quite out of the way and sits hidden within the Snowdonia mountains. In 1911 a 35ft high dam was constructed at the eastern end of Llyn Eigiau to supply water for the Dolgarrog power station. Due to alleged corer cutting, the dam burst in 1925 and water flooded down to a nearby reservoir causing that to burst also. Millions of gallons of water flowed into Dolgarrog and 16 people lost their lives. You can view what remains of the dam today and see where the dam broke. The drive up to the lake is narrow and on a single track lane through multiple gates (make sure to close them behind you). Although you can't drive straight to the lake, there is a car park ½ a mile away to allow you to walk down.

WWW.SNOWDONIAGUIDE.COM/LLYN_EIGIAU

20. Zip World Fforest

Nestled in the Conwy Valley, Zip World Fforest offers an idyllic woodland setting for adventures galore. Although the coaster has been mentioned already, there are plenty more activities on offer at the Zip World Fforest which may also entice you. Ziplines, rope swings, tree top nets and more are on offer for all ages. You could try Europe's highest giant swing, Skyride, if you dare!

WWW.ZIPWORLD.CO.UK/LOCATION/FFOREST

21. Walk around Llyn Brenig

Llyn Brenig is a large artificial reservoir 1,200 ft above sea level in the Denbigh Moors. The large lake offers a relatively flat walk around it. The Brenig Trail circles Llyn Brenig through forest and along the shoreline of the lake. Most of the route is on off-road tracks with one short section along a B-road and one climb. The route is suitable for both family cycling and for walking at 9.5 miles long. There is a visitor centre as well for hiring bikes or water activities.

LLYNBRENIG.COM

22. Have a ride on the toboggan on the Great Orme

Take a ride the longest Cresta Toboggan run in Wales! At an amazing 575m long, you don't want to miss this exhilarating experience. Fantastic fun for the young and old. It encircles the ski slope and gives off great views of the town of Llandudno whilst you fly down. You get two runs per ticket which is definitely enough fun to enjoy.

WWW.JNLLLANDUDNO.CO.UK/SLOPES/TUBING-TOBOGGANING/

23. Walk up to Aber Falls

Abergwyngregyn was an important dwelling place for the Princes of Gwynedd, and archaeological remains suggest that man has lived in this area since pre-historic times, over 2000 years ago. Rhaeadr Fawr (Aber Falls) and the Aber plantation epitomise Snowdonia's heritage and nature, and the path to the falls passes through the natural habitat of many local plants and trees. Wandering along the path, you will get a glimpse of Snowdonia's wildlife, native plants and beautiful views, including Rhaeadr Fawr. At around 2 miles long, this walk can be steep and challenging, but definitely rewarding. The car parks can fill quickly and it's advised to avoid driving through the town and parking lower down.

WALK-SNOWDONIA.CO.UK/RABER.PHP

24. Get soaked while white water rafting

With about 9km of natural river, the National White Water Centre, near Bala in North Wales, is the only commercially rafted stretch of water in the UK that compares to whitewater rafting worldwide. The Tryweryn river mixes the intensity of an Olympic-grade whitewater course and a journey through the Snowdonia National Park – it has the highest density of otters in North Wales. Plus it's a beautiful river.

WWW.NATIONALWHITEWATERCENTRE.CO.UK

25. Avoid the crowds up Moel Siabod

As Snowdon is the more famous and popular walk in North Wales, that brings with it the problems of becoming very busy during the summer months. One way to avoid the crowds is to tackle a smaller nearby mountain which allows you to look over to Snowdon, whilst being more secluded. The walk up Moel Siabod is an up and down the same path route, starting from Plas Y Brenin and working through the trees until it begins to climb more steeply. At the top the path can disappear in the rocks, but you want to continue to climb higher and the peak itself will emerge. Make sure to take a compass and map and suitable clothing and equipment, don't attempt in cloudy or bad weather as visibility can be poor at the top and never be afraid to turn around. On a clear day though, the view at the top is stunning. Make sure to try and spot Snowdon whilst up there!

WWW.ALLTRAILS.COM/TRAIL/WALES/CONWY/MOEL-SIABOD-FROM-PLAS-Y-BRENIN

Exploring

This section delves into the less activity based things to do, and more on the attractions of North Wales. These may include places to visit and the more and less well known tourist attractions that are definitely worth a visit.

There are places that delve into the history of North Wales, some allow you to see the magnificent views of North Wales and some are just a delight to visit and enjoy.

Map - Exploring

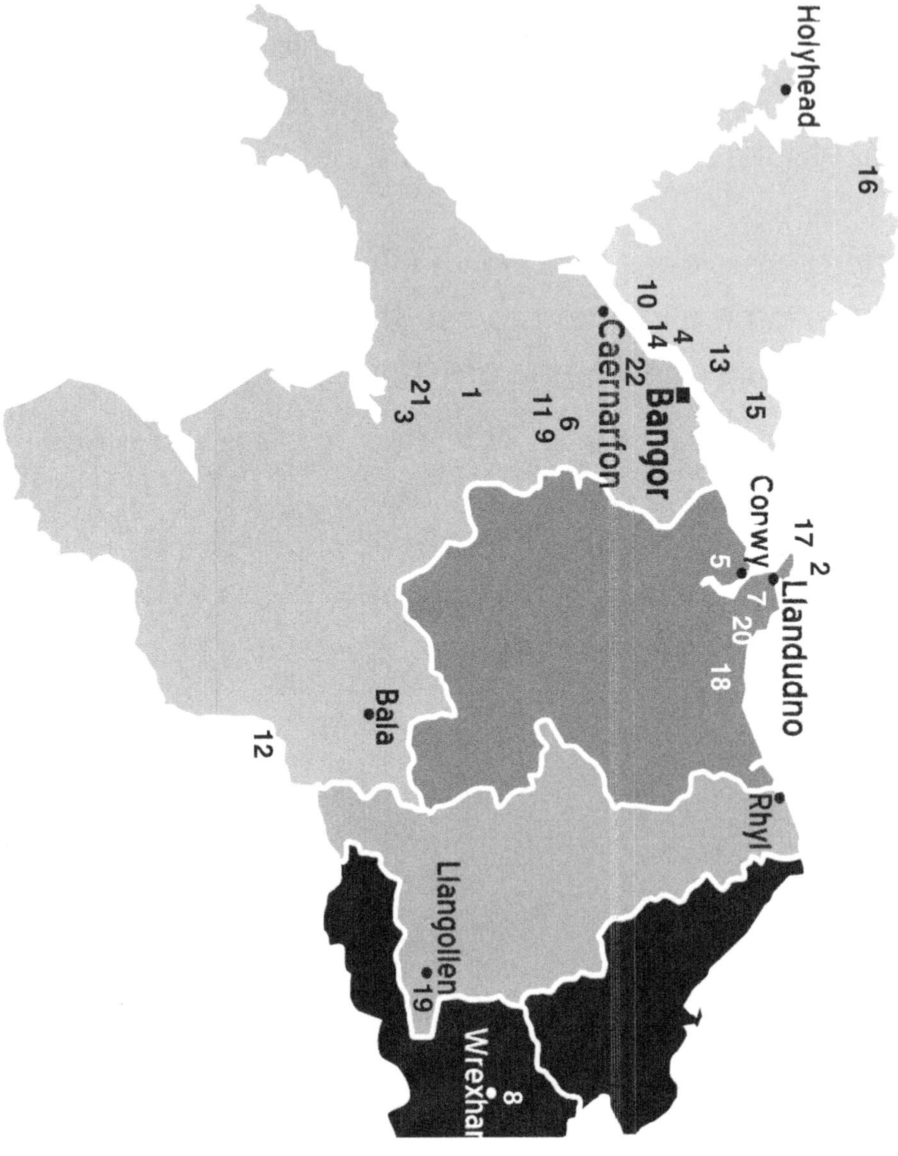

1. Discover the Legend Of Gelert and explore Beddgelert

The charming and tranquil town of Beddgelert hidden neatly in the heart of Snowdonia exemplifies a North Wales village. The town, which claims to be named after a legendary and noble hound named Gelert and his story, which dates back to medieval times. The story is a well-known and beloved variation on a folktale of many different cultures: a loyal and true canine companion falsely accused of taking a life. The picturesque stone-built village is the ideal base for exploring all the classic sights and beauty spots – Aberglaslyn Pass to the south, Nant Gwynant to the east, Snowdon to the north.

WWW.NATIONALTRUST.ORG.UK/CRAFLWYN-AND-BEDDGELERT/TRAILS/GELERTS-GRAVE-WALK-BEDDGELERT

2. Cable cars up the Great Orme

Situated on the peak of the Great Orme in Llandudno, the cable cars installed in 1969 still run to this day. They will take you from Happy Valley up to the summit, where you will be able to take in the stunning views Bay of Llandudno, the Little Orme, the Conwy Estuary and miles out over the Irish Sea. And then look down on the beautiful gardens of Happy Valley or glimpse the action on the Llandudno Ski Slope. The cable car doesn't operate during high winds, and only takes cash payments, so make sure to bring cash to not be disappointed!

WWW.LLANDUDNO.COM/LLANDUDNO-CABLE-CARS/

3. Explore the famous colourful town of Portmeirion

Be instantaneously transported to a charming Italianate village, whilst remaining in the heart of North Wales. Portmeirion Village is one of Wales' most popular attractions! Where Wales meets Italy, Portmeirion is a picture-perfect village, that could easily be mistaken for a Mediterranean holiday destination. Discover colourful façades, an elaborate piazza, ornate gardens and breathtaking scenery at Portmeirion Village. There are plenty of things to do in Portmeirion, and it's easy to spend at least a full day here. Portmeirion is definitely not to be missed, as it's beautiful sights aren't given justice in pictures. Also, if you're around this area at the start of September, check out Festival No. 6, an art and music festival held in Portmeirion which presents a wide range of music genres across multiple stages.

PORTMEIRION.WALES

4. Try and pronounce the famous welsh town Llanfairpwllgwyngyllgogerychwyrndrobwllllantysiliogogogoch Train Station

The railway station in the village of Llanfairpwll is one of the great curiosities of Wales, a gimmick-heavy spot that you should try and see if you're in the area. There isn't much here other than the various signs, all of which are immensely photogenic and will keep your head spinning for hours on end.

TFW.WALES/PLACES/STATIONS/LLANFAIRPWLL

5. Smallest house in Britain

The Smallest House in Great Britain can be found nestled at the end of a terrace of houses on Conwy's quayside. You really can't miss the smallest house and you'd be crazy not to pop in for a look on your way past. This national treasure is well worth a few minutes of your time. The visitors are impressed by the very special atmosphere of the house inside - visitors also enjoy a short history of the property.

WWW.THESMALLESTHOUSE.CO.UK

6. Summit Snowdon without walking on the Snowdon Mountain Railway

Since 1896 visitors have been travelling to Llanberis, to experience the unique rail journey to the Summit of the highest mountain in Wales and England. Experience exactly why Snowdon Mountain Railway has been described as one of the most unique and wonderful railway journeys in the world. If you're looking to enjoy all the sights and scenery of Snowdon in a more relaxing fashion, then this is the train for you!

SNOWDONRAILWAY.CO.UK

7. Walk along Llandudno Pier

Few things say 'seaside holiday' quite like a stroll along the pier, and Llandudno Pier is a real gem! With its Grade II listed status, it's a traditional seaside pier dating from the late 1800s with an array of shops, cafes, bars and attractions – offering fun for all the family! Stretching 2,295 feet (700 m) over the sea, Llandudno Pier is the longest in Wales, and one of the UK's finest. The Pier houses arcades, gift shops, bars and funfair rides, with something for everyone to enjoy.

WWW.LLANDUDNOPIER.COM

8. Support oldest football team in Wales at Wrexham FC

Formed in 1864, Wrexham FC is the oldest football club in Wales and the second oldest professional association football team in the world! Watch a bit of history in motion and support the team at their home ground in Wrexham if a game is scheduled. The club has recently transferred to new Hollywood owners, Ryan Reynolds and Rob McElhenney, who want to bring the team back up the higher leagues. The club has a lot of history, and although it currently sits in the National League, the fifth tier of the English football league system, it's still great to enjoy a match of history.

WWW.WREXHAMAFC.CO.UK

9. Learn some history in the National Slate Museum

Shadowed by towering slate mountains, the National Slate Museum Llanberis is housed in the Industrial Victorian Workshops that once serviced and maintained the enormous Dinorwig slate quarry above it. The workshops catered for all the repair and maintenance work demanded by a quarry, which once employed well over 3,000 men. From strikes and suffering to craftsmanship and community, this is a unique opportunity to glimpse the lives of the slate workers and their families. The museum has free entry and allows you to explore and learn about a once forgotten industry which kept this area alive!

MUSEUM.WALES/SLATE/

10. Anglesey Sea Zoo

Bring the family along to visit Seahorses, Octopus, Lobsters and other exciting elusive British marine animals up close. Lose yourself in the moon jellyfish display, or spot the Conger Eels as you enter the Seven Sisters shipwreck or take a seat in front of the largest tank of silvery bass, bream and wrasse. It's hypnotic! The aquarium also has its very own gift shop and a Rockpool Café which serves a wide selection of drinks, snacks and meals. If that isn't enough, there's a children's play area, crazy golf and the zoo is right on Anglesey's Coastal Path to guarantee a splashing day out.

WWW.ANGLESEYSEAZOO.CO.UK

11. Ride the steam train around Llyn Padarn

This lovely little train line runs alongside Llyn Padarn in the Llanberis for a there-and-back journey of five miles. Stop off for a lakeside picnic at Cei Llydan and enjoy the sights of Snowdonia. You won't need a head for heights to enjoy great views of Snowdon on this Llanberis stream train. The five mile return trip takes around 60 minutes, and all advertised trains are scheduled to be hauled by one of the vintage steam engines rescued from the nearby Dinorwic slate quarries.

WWW.LAKE-RAILWAY.CO.UK

12. Spa Day in Lake Vyrnwy hotel

Sometimes you need to have a day of relaxation when on holiday. In North Wales there are lots of activities and adventures to go on, so it's important to balance these out with some targeted relaxation. That's where Lake Vyrnwy Hotel & Spa comes in. Sitting with beautiful views over the lake and the surrounding countryside, this Hotel & Spa will make sure that you leave relaxed and rejuvenated and ready to tackle any more adventures that North Wales may throw at you. Make sure to book in advance to avoid disappointment.
www.lakevyrnwy.com

13. Pili Palas

Family days out on Anglesey at Pili Palas can be a magical experience for all the family - whatever the weather! Enter a steamy environment full of lush vegetation and waterfalls with live butterflies flying all around you. This is the magical world of Pili Palas. There's a lot more than just butterflies to see as well, you'll meet a host of other feathered friends in the birdhouse as well. There are plenty of snakes and lizards of all kinds for you to get up close to if you want to. If someone likes bugs, then they'll have the time of their life in the bug-zone - home to hissing cockroaches, millipedes, locusts, giant snails and much more. Don't forget pets' corner where you can meet the rabbits and guinea pigs. Take a walk through the farmyard where pygmy goats live happily with the gorgeous Kune Kune pigs.

WWW.PILIPALAS.CO.UK

14. Plas Newydd

Plas Newydd is a beautiful country house set in gardens and parklands on the north bank of the Menai Straits. As a national trust venue, there is a long and rich history spanning hundreds of years behind this lovely location. You're able to explore the gardens and beautiful mansion for a whole day of things to do and see for the whole family. Tickets to the National Trust venue are around £28 for a family for the house and gardens.

WWW.NATIONALTRUST.ORG.UK/PLAS-NEWYDD-HOUSE-AND-GARDEN

15. Visit the seaside town of Beaumaris

Beaumaris is a captivating seaside town, with its mix of medieval, Georgian, Victorian and Edwardian architecture. Its name is based on the Norman 'beau marais', meaning 'fair marsh', a description of the site chosen by Edward 1 for the last of his 'Iron ring' of castles, constructed in his bid to control the Welsh. A 'must' is to take a walk through the town, starting with a stroll along the seafront, taking in the pier and the views over the Menai Strait and Snowdonia then continuing through the charming streets with their picturesque cottages, many painted in soft pastel colours.
www.beaumaris.com

16. Try and find wildlife at Cemlyn Bay Lagoon

A real wildlife haven with a spectacular seabird colony at its heart. A visit to Cemlyn is filled with possibility – you never know what might turn up! Situated on the north coast of Anglesey, Cemlyn is an incredible site to visit. The ridge is an important habitat for specialist plant species. Beyond the ridge, the lagoon is an interesting habitat for aquatic species, whilst surrounding areas of grassland provide habitat for a wide range of butterflies and birds. The site is best visited from May through to July when the islands within the lagoon host the nesting colonies of terns. It is the only nesting colony of Sandwich terns in Wales and a true wildlife spectacle – not to be missed!

WWW.NORTHWALESWILDLIFETRUST.ORG.UK/NATURE-RESERVES/CEMLYN

17. Explore The Great Orme

The Great Orme in Llandudno is home to many things to see and do. The Great Orme is Llandudno's mini-mountain and it's rich in natural and man-made history. You really can't miss it. The Great Orme headland is a massive chunk of limestone that rises 679ft straight out of the sea. Little wonder that its name, given by the Vikings, means 'sea monster'. You can drive or walk around the one way toll road called Marine Drive, which allows you to enjoy beautiful views of the Irish Sea, Anglsey, Puffin Island and Snowdonia. You can also explore the copper mine that sits inside the heart of the Great Orme, take a ride on the historic tram and take in the beautiful views from the summit.

WWW.VISITCONWY.ORG.UK/EXPLORE/OUTDOORS/GREAT-ORME-COUNTRY-PARK

18. Welsh Mountain Zoo

The National Zoo of Wales is an education and conservation charity, home to a wide range of rare and endangered animals, from brown bears to sea lions, red-faced spiders to snow leopards. The gardens around the zoo are awash with tropical and local plants providing a diverse backdrop full of colour and life. For children who want to practice their Tarzan antics, there's the jungle adventure land suitable for all ages and the Tarzan trail! Stop for a snack on The Safari Restaurant balcony, which overlooks the tiger enclosure or try The Penguin Café and dine with your flippered friends instead!

WWW.WELSHMOUNTAINZOO.ORG

19. Take in an engineering marvel at Pontcysyllte Aqueduct

The Pontcysyllte Aqueduct is a spectacular example of canal engineering in the late eighteenth and early nineteenth centuries, encompassing an architectural masterpiece in a dramatic landscape setting. Its nineteen cast-iron spans carry the waterway 126 feet above the river, and for two centuries it remained the tallest navigable aqueduct in the world. You can walk across the Aqueduct for free and enjoy this marvellous UNESCO world heritage site. There is plenty of things to enjoy in the surrounding areas too, such as the picturesque town of Llangollen, Cefn Viaduct, Chirk Castle and Valle Crucis Abbey. At least a day of enjoyment can be had in this area.

WWW.PONTCYSYLLTE-AQUEDUCT.CO.UK

20. Catch a show in Venue Cymru

While in North Wales, why not try and catch a show in the heart of Llandudno. There are all varieties of shows on, whether it be a comedian, rock music show, theatre performance or even a family workshop to get creative with the whole family. Take a look at the website and see what's on during your visit.

WWW.VENUECYMRU.CO.UK

21. Ffestiniog & Welsh Highland Railway

The historic Ffestiniog Railway climbs from sea level to over 700ft on its journey through the mountainous Snowdonia National Park and round the UK's only railway spiral to the 'slate capital' of Blaenau Ffestiniog. The recently reopened Welsh Highland Railway is the UK's longest narrow gauge railway - an epic 25 mile mountain adventure through the alpine scenery of the Aberglaslyn Pass to the historic castle town of Caernarfon. Your ticket will entitle you to your own compartment on a carriage with prices starting from £50 per compartment, which includes the fare for 2 adults. Tickets for each additional adult cost £25, while the fare for each child will be £1.

WWW.FESTRAIL.CO.UK

22. Family fun at Greenwood Family Park

A forest of family fun and great outdoor adventure awaits at the award-winning GreenWood Family Park; a gigantic playground nestled beneath the trees of Snowdonia's National Park full of amusement, magic and mischief. Dotted amongst the woodland floor you'll discover an enchanting world powered by people... make a splash on the UK's only solar powered water ride, jump aboard the world's first people powered roller coaster and zoom down the longest sledge run in Wales! The park is open over summer from April and closes in winter. Tickets sit at around £20 per person.

WWW.GREENWOODFAMILYPARK.CO.UK

Castles

North Wales is famous for its centuries old Castles dotted along the coast. Many of them built during the late 13th century by King Edward I to secure North Wales following the death of Llywelyn ap Grufford in 1282.

He built a series of castles to fortify and defend the area to ensure that the Welsh did not trouble him again. In 1276–77 and 1282–83, King Edward I led two military campaigns in Wales to defeat the Welsh princes and bring Wales under English rule. To do this, between 1276 and 1295 many castles were built or repaired.

This section of the guide will cover some of the great castles of North Wales that are well worth a visit. It would definitely be a shame to visit North Wales and not experience these immense castles in person.

Map - Castles

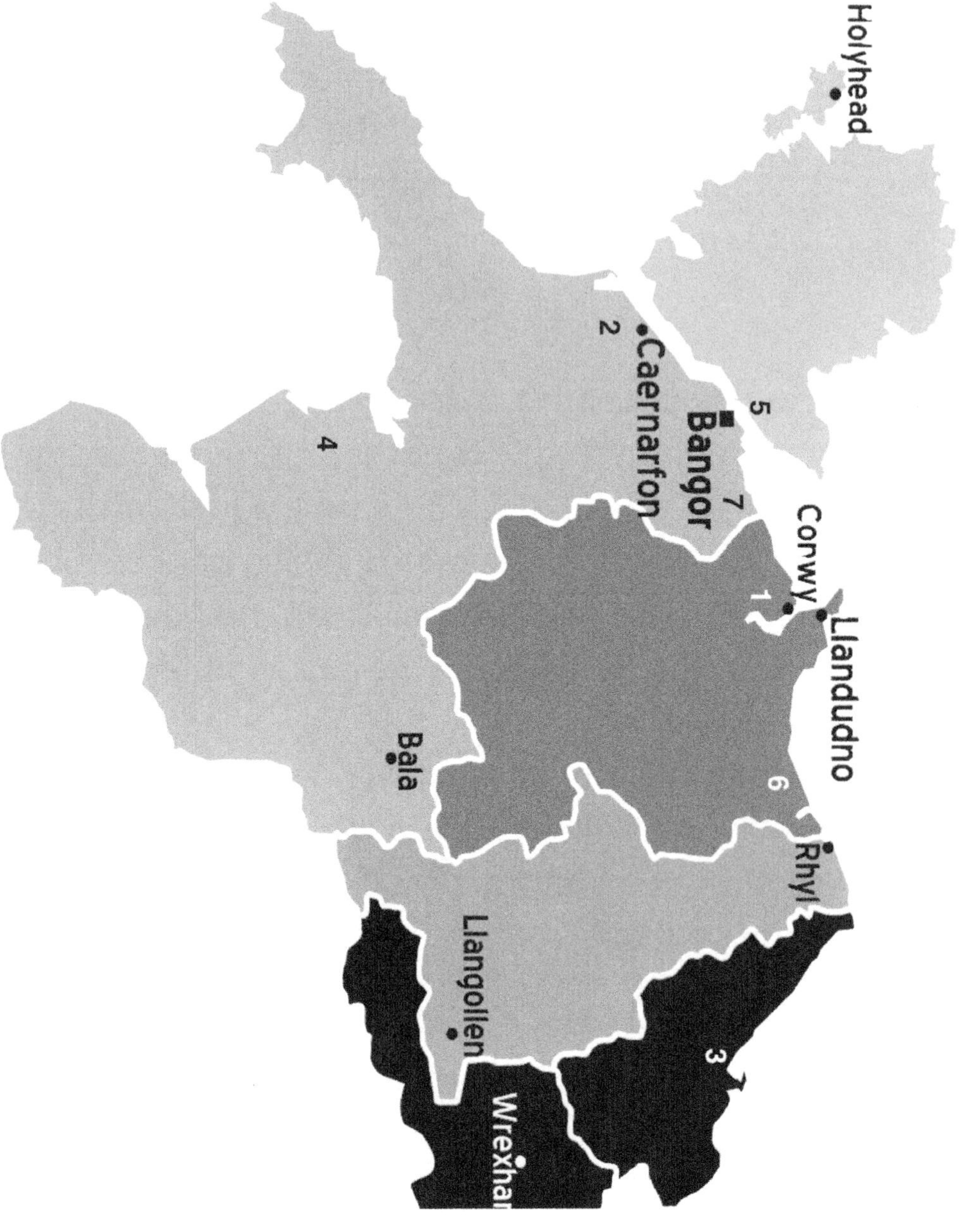
Holyhead
2
Caernarfon
5
Bangor
7
4
Conwy
1
Llandudno
Bala
6
Rhyl
Llangollen
3

1. Conwy Castle

Conwy Castle, set against the mountains of Snowdonia is as impressive today as it was 700 years ago. Construction of the castle was finished in 1287, having taken a little over four years to complete. The town and castle of Conwy were built as a single entity. While exploring the castle, make sure to also walk along the surrounding walls to really take in the history of this town.

CADW.GOV.WALES/VISIT/PLACES-TO-VISIT/CONWY-CASTLE

2. Caernarfon Castle

Caernarfon Castle is recognised around the world as one of the greatest buildings of the Middle Ages. This fortress-palace on the banks of the River Seiont is grouped with Edward I's other castles at Conwy, Beaumaris and Harlech as a World Heritage Site. But for sheer scale and architectural drama Caernarfon stands alone. Here Edward and his military architect Master James of St George erected a castle, town walls and a quay all at the same time. This gigantic building project eventually took 47 years and cost a staggering £25,000 (£30 million today).

CADW.GOV.WALES/VISIT/PLACES-TO-VISIT/CAERNARFON-CASTLE

3. Flint Castle

Fans of military architecture make a bee-line for Flint. The first castle to be founded as part Edward I's campaign against Llywelyn ap Gruffydd in north Wales, it boasts a unique and unusually sophisticated design. Started in 1277 and largely completed by 1284, the castle is dominated by the great tower (or donjon) at its south-east corner. Surrounded by its own moat and accessed via a drawbridge, it's essentially a castle within a castle. Built with exceptionally thick walls and equipped with all the facilities required to withstand a siege, it was presumably intended to be a final refuge in the event of an attack. Admission is free. Most of the castle has been destroyed during the Civil War in 1646, so only the ruins remain to be explored.

CADW.GOV.WALES/VISIT/PLACES-TO-VISIT/FLINT-CASTLE

4. Harlech Castle

None of Edward I's mighty coastal fortresses has a more spectacular setting. Harlech Castle crowns a sheer rocky crag overlooking the dunes far below – waiting in vain for the tide to turn and the distant sea to lap at its feet once again. No further drama is really required but, just in case, the rugged peaks of Snowdonia rise as a backdrop. This is probably the most spectacular setting for any of Edward I's castles in North Wales. An extremely well defendable castle that still looks fierce to this day.

CADW.GOV.WALES/VISIT/PLACES-TO-VISIT/HARLECH-CASTLE

5. Beaumaris Castle

Beaumaris castle is famous as the greatest castle never built. It was the last of the royal strongholds created by Edward I – and perhaps his masterpiece. Here Edward and his architect took full advantage of the blank canvas beside the Menai Strait. By now they'd already constructed the great castles of Conwy, Caernarfon and Harlech. This was to be their crowning glory. The result was a fortress of immense size and near-perfect symmetry. The outer walls alone bristled with 300 arrow loops. But lack of money and trouble in Scotland meant building work had petered out by the 1320s. The six great towers in the inner ward never reached their intended height, although not totally finished, it is still a marvel to walk around and learn about.

CADW.GOV.WALES/VISIT/PLACES-TO-VISIT/BEAUMARIS-CASTLE

6. Gwyrch Castle

Gwrych Castle is a Grade I listed 19th-century country house near Abergele in Conwy. The castle is privately owned and stands in over 240 acres of gardens & grounds with extensive views over former parkland including a deer park and the Irish Sea. Gwrych Castle was built between 1810 and 1825 by Lloyd Hesketh Bamford-Hesketh. It is also famous now due to its association with the TV show 'I'm a Celebrity…' which has celebrities competing in challenges to try and win. You can visit the grounds and gardens, or even go on a ghost hunt!

WWW.GWRYCHCASTLE.CO.UK

7. Penrhyn Castle

This enormous 19th-century neo-Norman castle sits between Snowdonia and the Menai Strait. It's crammed with fascinating items, such as a one-ton slate bed made for Queen Victoria, elaborate carvings, plasterwork and mock-Norman furniture. It also has an outstanding collection of paintings. The restored kitchens are a delight and the stable block houses a fascinating industrial railway museum and a model railway museum. The 24.3 hectares (60 acres) of grounds include parkland, an exotic tree and shrub collection as well as a Victorian walled garden.

WWW.NATIONALTRUST.ORG.UK/PENRHYN-CASTLE

Food & drink

With 1000's of places to eat and drink in North Wales, there's no I could ever fit them all into this small guide! In which case, I have hand picked a few of my favourites that you should try.

There are plenty of restaurant specific guides online which will go into unbelievable detail about your specific area which are definitely worth exploring if you have the time.

However, if you're looking for my local recommendations, then look no further than this next section.

Map - Food & drink

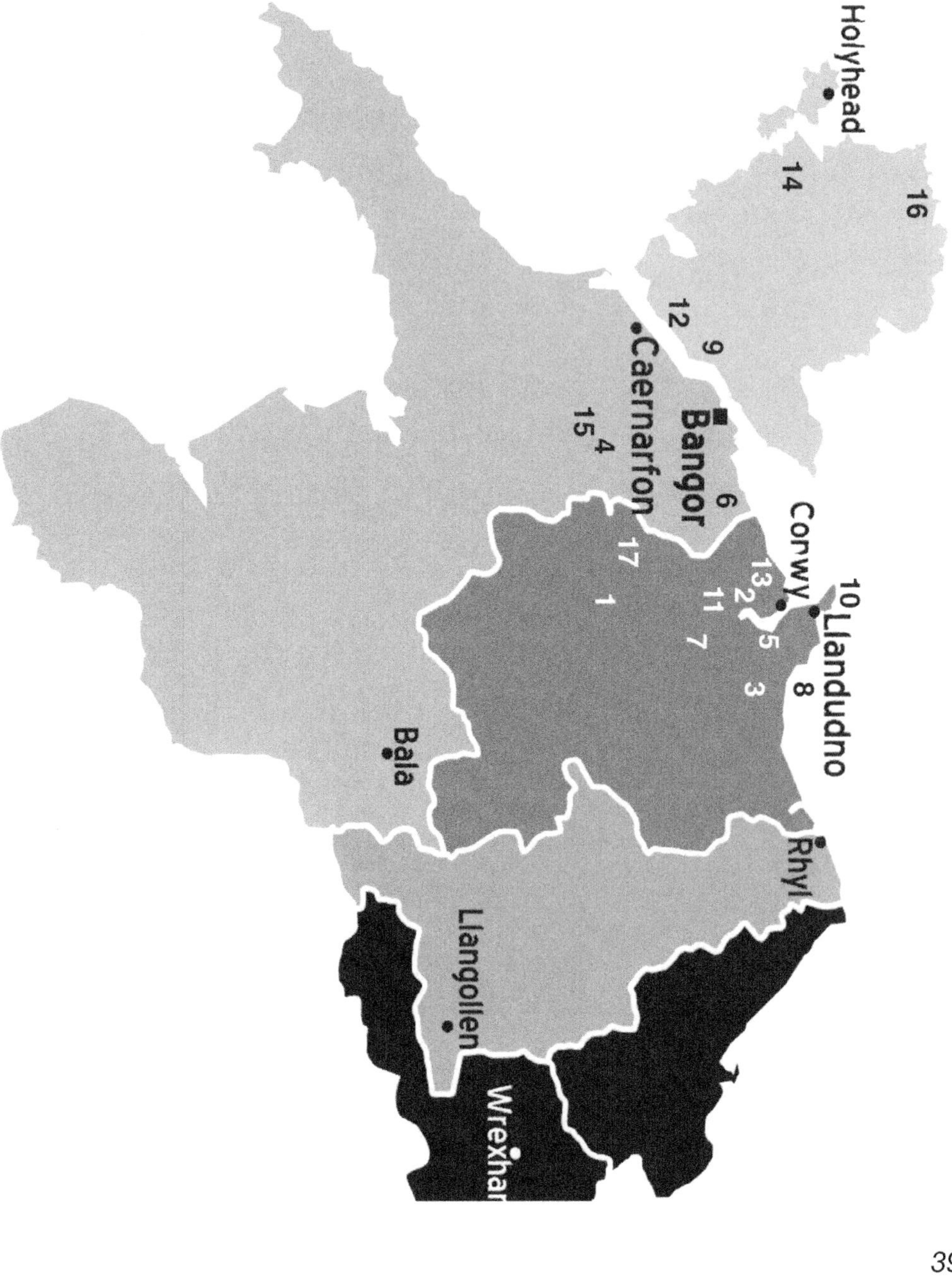

1. Tu Hwnt i'r Bont - tearoom

One of Wales's most photographed places is situated in the village of Llanrwst. Covered in ivy, Tu Hwnt i'r Bont tea room is awash in colour most of the year, transforming from a vibrant spring green to a fiery red in the autumn. The tea room menu includes plenty of Welsh classics like bara brith and bakestones. The tea room itself is actually a 500 year old building which sits beautifully next to the Afon Conwy river.

WWW.TUHWNTIRBONT.CO.UK

2. Conwy real ale trail

Spend a day rediscovering the charm of authentic Welsh pubs and unique Welsh real ales, without having to worry about who's driving! The trail takes you to some of the best pubs and microbreweries, found in the villages dotted around Conwy County. The route is always changing – new pubs and new ales are added to every trail, so there's always something new to experience. Check the dates of the trails to ensure you don't miss it, as it only happens once every few months! However, if you do miss the actual event, you can always retrace the steps yourself instead using the local buses and public transport.

REALALETRAIL.CO.UK/CONWY-REAL-ALE-TRAIL/

3. Tour of Conwy Brewery

This guided brewery tour offers a great insight into the beer making process. Embark on a tour of one of North Wales' top breweries - winners of the first ever Beer Academy Welsh Pale Ale award in 2012. Learn all about their delicate production process, from the preparation of raw ingredients, right through to the bottling of the finished product. Learn about seasonal ales such as St. David's Ale and heritage ales like Telford Porter, which is linked to the history of Conwy.

WWW.CONWYBREWERY.CO.UK

4. Refuel at Pete's Eats in Llanberis

Pete's Eats is a cafe in Llanberis, North Wales, popular amongst walkers and climbers in the Snowdonia region of mountains. Llanberis, at the foot of Snowdon, is one of the traditional starting points for climbs in the Snowdonia National Park. The Cafe has long been an important centre for climbers, described as "one of the most famous mountaineering hangouts in Britain". It even received a small mention in the New York Times as "cheap and filling" and "rowdy fun".

WWW.PETES-EATS.CO.UK

5. Fine dining or afternoon tea at Bodysgallen hall

A magnificent stone and slate building that started life as a five-storey medieval tower, this National Trust property balances abundant period features (grand fireplaces, wood panelling, brooding oil paintings) with sensible modern touches – including a spa and tennis courts in its 200 acres of grounds. Food-wise, take your pick from the informal Bistro 1620 or the more traditional restaurant (chandeliers, mullioned windows et al), where the cooking is intelligent, inventive and driven by flavour.

WWW.BODYSGALLEN.COM/WINE-DINE/

6. Aber Falls Distillery

Aber Falls Whisky Distillery is one of only four in Wales, and the first in North Wales since the early 1900s. Located within a stone's throw of Rhaeadr Fawr, the famous Aber Falls waterfall, the whisky is distilled, bottled and matured in the distillery, using specially crafted Welsh ingredients from the surrounding area. With whisky available from 2021, they also have a premium range of small batch, handcrafted gins and liqueurs. The Visitor Centre is open for tours of the distillery and your chance to experience the skill and passion that goes into Aber Falls spirits.

WWW.ABERFALLSDISTILLERY.COM/EN/

7. Bodnant Welsh Food Centre

The Bodnant Welsh Food Centre is a true culinary delight. You can buy locally produced food in the farm shop, including a butcher and bakery. You can also eat at the excellent Hayloft Restaurant or Furnace Tea Room. There's even the possibility of having a go yourself at the Cookery or Wine school available at the location. If you're looking for a taste of North Wales, this is the place to be. If you love honey, come and learn all about the bees and why they are so important to those at the National Beekeeping Centre of Wales based in the courtyard. There are plenty of events here if you are looking for things to do in North Wales whilst on holiday.

WWW.BODNANT-WELSHFOOD.CO.UK

8. Bryn Williams at Porth Eirias

A stones throw away from the sea and the stunning beach of Porth Eirias lies Bryn Williams' bistro. The menu is full of Welsh produce that have been produced as local as possible. This big open space with its easy, informal mood has an open kitchen where Bryn's team of chefs turn simple, local, seasonal ingredients into extraordinary bistro-style food. Seafood takes centre stage on the menu from prawns, cod to mussels, something for everyone's taste!

PORTHEIRIAS.COM

9. Dylan's Restaurant on the Menai Straits

Dylan's is nestled in to the banks of the Menai with stunning views over this coastal haven. The restaurants modern boatyard theme, both inside and out allows it to blend in perfectly with the natural environment of the area. Plush, lush and discrete. Menai bridge has to be a favourite due to its location, it's literally over the sea. The local scenery is amazing and there is just something calming about the little boats as they pass. Rain or shine it is an area of outstanding beauty, where better to enjoy some of the fantastic local produce they have to offer. Making a booking is highly recommended especially during the summer holiday season, there is also parking available a short walk away.

DYLANSRESTAURANT.CO.UK/RESTAURANT/LOCATIONS/MENAI-BRIDGE

10. Kings Head

The 300-year-old King's Head is the oldest inn in Llandudno. It has a traditional split level bar dominated by a large open fire and a grill restaurant at the rear. The pub makes an ideal stop after walking on the Great Orme or riding on Britain's only cable-hauled tramway. A very traditional pub will welcome all those who come to visit, whether it be for some proper pub grub, or simply to have a drink and enjoy the atmosphere.

RESTAURANTGURU.COM/KINGS-HEAD-LLANDUDNO

11. The Groes Inn - 500 year old pub

The Groes Inn is an independent 500 year old hotel and restaurant with rustic soul by the bucket-load. Overlooking the lush Conwy Estuary, the country-cosy Inn is blessed with stunning views, award-winning dining and a well-groomed bar. Bringing the 'traditional coaching inn' bang-up-to-date, The Groes' handsome bedrooms are kitted out with all the mod cons. Awarded AA Pub of the Year, it's just the kind of place you'll be looking for after a day out exploring Conwy or hiking in the hills! Perfectly situated for all major North Wales attractions. Bodnant Garden 1 mile, Conwy town 2 miles.

WWW.GROESINN.COM

12. Halen mon

The Anglesey family food business making the world's finest sea salt. Halen Môn Welsh sea salt is sold worldwide and in over 100 of the best UK delicatessens, plus on the shelves of some of the nation's best regarded chain food stores. It may seem strange why a salt maker is on this list, but the salt really is special and it doesn't get more local and natural than straight from the Menai Straits! They also offer tours around their site to discover how they make the salt!

WWW.HALENMON.COM

13. Signatures of Conwy

For the finest in British cuisine, professional and friendly service book into Signatures Restaurant and Bar. Owned and managed by Executive Chef Jimmy Williams, he has created one of the best dining experiences on the North Wales coast. The contemporary surroundings lend to the theatre style kitchen, which allows you to view the chef and his, highly trained, team prepare your freshly made dishes. As winners of the Best Welsh Restaurant, Executive Chef Jimmy creates all the mouth watering dishes and tweaks the menu on a regular basis, giving plenty of variety to all.

DARWINESCAPES.CO.UK/ABERCONWY-RESORT-SPA/FACILITIES/SIGNATURES-RESTAURANT/

14. Sea Shanty Cafe

The Sea Shanty café sits among the marram grass at the edge of Trearddur Bay's golden crescent of sand. It's no surprise the Sea Shanty celebrates the village's maritime history, with actual rowing boats hanging from the beams. It's open all day until 9pm, seven days a week for coffee and cakes, ice creams, and inventive main courses featuring local delicacies. Not to be missed: Breakfast. If you're are planning a walk on the Wales Coast Path that virtually passes the door, a plate of smoked salmon and scrambled eggs should set you up nicely.

SEASHANTYCAFE.CO.UK

15. Georgio's Ice Cream in Llanberis

Don't be put off by the website of this small ice cream parlour based in Llanberis. The ice cream you can get here is some of the nicest I have ever tried. On a sweltering summers day, after paddling in Llyn Padarn or walking through Snowdonia, an ice cream here just hits like nothing else. They make all of the ice cream on the premises themselves, so you can rest assured you're getting real local ice cream.

GEORGIOSICECREAM.CO.UK

16. Enjoy the freshest milkshakes you can buy (probably) at Llefrith Nant Dairy

Sitting in a small wooden hut in a lay-by on Anglesey is some of the best milkshake you can try. With the idea originating due to the Covid lockdowns, the Nant y Fran dairy farm decided to stock a vending machine with very fresh and creamy milkshakes directly from the farm. Nant y Fran is a dairy farm run by a young local family. The farm has around 300 Fresian cows, milked in the most sustainable way possible. The cattle graze for the majority of the year and produce high-quality milk. To maintain the natural taste the milk is not homogenised just gently pasteurised.The standard flavours of milkshake are banana, strawberry and chocolate. In addition, there will be one extra flavour each week, announced on the board at the vending machines. All ingredients for the milkshakes are also listed.

CEMAES.WALES/ORGANISATION/LLEFRITH-NANT-DAIRY/

17. Grab a Siabod breakfast at Siabod Cafe

Situated in the centre of Capel Curig in the heart of Snowdonia The Moel Siabod Café opened its doors in Spring 2012. Seeking to provide excellent food & drinks at a reasonable price with a warm & friendly welcome they hope to bring something new to the experience of North Wales. Their love of Snowdonia makes them want to help you enjoy this beautiful location by encouraging you to get out there & enjoy the surroundings.

WWW.MOELSIABODCAFE.CO.UK

End of guide

Thank you for reading, I hope you found the guide useful for you and I hope that your time in North Wales is something that you enjoy.

Author Bio

Dylan Thomas, although sharing the name with the famous poet, is unfortunately not a poet, but certainly enjoys writing! Raised in Llandudno, North Wales, he has created this guide to help all visitors to the region. He has spent decades enjoying the Welsh countryside and visiting the best that North Wales has to offer. Hopefully this transfers well to a locally written guide for those who want to come and enjoy the region.

Printed in Great Britain
by Amazon

14242886R00037